Ephesians

D1495624

Back to the Bible Study Guides

Judges: Ordinary People, Extraordinary God

Proverbs: The Pursuit of God's Wisdom

John: Face-to-Face with Jesus

James: Living Your Faith

Revelation: The Glorified Christ

EPHESIANS

LIFE IN GOD'S FAMILY

WOODROW KROLL

CROSSWAY BOOKS

A PUBLISHING MINISTRY OF
GOOD NEWS PUBLISHERS
WHEATON, ILLINOIS

Ephesians: Life in God's Family

Copyright © 2007 by Back to the Bible

Published by Crossway Books
           a publishing ministry of Good News Publishers
           1300 Crescent Street
           Wheaton, Illinois 60187

All rights reserved. No part of this publication may be reproduced, stored in a retrieval system, or transmitted in any form by any means, electronic, mechanical, photocopy, recording, or otherwise, without the prior permission of the publisher, except as provided by USA copyright law.

Cover design: Josh Dennis

Cover photo: iStock

First printing, 2007

Printed in the United States of America

ISBN 13: 978-1-58134-881-1
ISBN 10: 1-58134-881-9

Unless otherwise indicated, all Scripture quotations are taken from *The Holy Bible: English Standard Version®*. Copyright © 2001 by Crossway Bibles, a publishing ministry of Good News Publishers. Used by permission. All rights reserved.

Produced with the assistance of The Livingstone Corporation (www.LivingstoneCorp.com).

Editorial assistance: Neil Wilson

CH		17	16	15	14	13	12	11	10	09	08	07
15	14	13	12	11	10	9	8	7	6	5	4	3	2	1

Table of Contents

How to Use This Study 7

Lesson One: The Plan 9

Lesson Two: A Reason for Prayer 15

Lesson Three: Where Faith Meets Grace 21

Lesson Four: Who's in the Family? 27

Lesson Five: A Message in the Mystery 33

Lesson Six: A Life-Changing Prayer .39

Lesson Seven: A Life Tour 45

Lesson Eight: Spiritual Conditioning 51

Lesson Nine: More Walking 57

Lesson Ten: Tough Roles 63

Lesson Eleven: Honoring Christ 69

Lesson Twelve: Armed and Dangerous 75

Lesson Thirteen: A Living Tapestry .81

How to Use This Study

Your study of Ephesians will have maximum impact if you prayerfully read each day's Scripture passage. The entire text of the Book of Ephesians from the English Standard Version is included in the study, with the selected passage printed before each lesson's reading, so that everything you need is in one place. While we recommend reading the Scripture passage before you read the devotional, some have found it helpful to use the devotional as preparation for reading the Scripture. If you are unfamiliar with the English Standard Version (on which this series of studies is based), you might consider reading the devotional, followed by reading the passage again from a different Bible version. This will give you an excellent basis for considering the rest of the lesson.

After each devotional there are three sections designed to help you better understand and apply the lesson's Scripture passage.

Consider It—Several questions will help you unpack and reflect on the Scripture passage of the day. These could be used for a small group discussion.

Express It—Suggestions for turning the insights from the lesson into prayer.

Go Deeper—The nature of this study makes it important to see the Book of Ephesians in the context of other passages and insights from Scripture. This brief section will allow you to consider some of the implications of the day's passage for the central theme of the study (Life in God's Family) as well as the way it fits with the rest of Scripture.

The Plan

God has a plan. The world may look more or less chaotic, but God is in control. He knows what He's doing, and He knows where the world is going. He hasn't told us the whole plan, but He has told us enough to amaze us. One of the wonderful glimpses of God's plan is called the Book of Ephesians.

Ephesians 1:1–14

Greeting

1 Paul, an apostle of Christ Jesus by the will of God,

To the saints who are in Ephesus, and are faithful in Christ Jesus:

²Grace to you and peace from God our Father and the Lord Jesus Christ.

Spiritual Blessings in Christ

³Blessed be the God and Father of our Lord Jesus Christ, who has blessed us in Christ with every spiritual blessing in the heavenly places, ⁴even as he chose us in him before the foundation of the world, that we should be holy and blameless before him. In love ⁵he predestined us for adoption through Jesus Christ, according to the purpose of his will, ⁶to the praise of his glorious grace, with which he has blessed us in the Beloved. ⁷In him we have redemption through his blood, the forgiveness of our trespasses, according to the riches of his grace, ⁸which he lavished upon us, in all wisdom and insight ⁹making known to us the mystery of his will, according to his purpose, which he set forth in Christ ¹⁰as a plan for the fullness of time, to unite all things in him, things in heaven and things on earth.

> # Key Verse
>
> *As a plan for the fullness of time, to unite all things in him, things in heaven and things on earth* (Eph. 1:10).

¹¹In him we have obtained an inheritance, having been predestined according to the purpose of him who works all things according to the counsel of his will, ¹²so that we who were the first to hope in Christ might be to the praise of his glory. ¹³In him you also, when you heard the word of truth, the gospel of your salvation, and believed in him, were sealed with the promised Holy Spirit, ¹⁴who is the guarantee of our inheritance until we acquire possession of it, to the praise of his glory.

Go Deeper

Theological terms like "election" and "predestination" trace their origins to passages like Ephesians 1:1–14. The apostle Paul's use of these words should be understood in two ways. First, we need to read the words as ordinary language that the apostle expected his readers to understand. Election (God's choosing) is a pretty controversial subject, and that makes it even more remarkable that Paul jumps right into the subject in his letter to the Ephesians.

Apparently, election was not as controversial in Paul's mind as it may be in our minds today. Maybe that's because he understood it better. God had enlightened him with regard to what election really means, and much of the theological baggage that's been carried through the centuries with regard to election was not part of Paul's thinking.

(continued)

Go Deeper Continued . . .

Who are we as creatures to question or begrudge God's sovereign right to make choices about the outcome of His great tapestry in history? After all, He is the Weaver and it is His tapestry.

Second, when we think about election, adoption and predestination, we need to continuously see these concepts within the context of the love of God. God did the choosing and deciding based on love. He didn't have to do any of this. None of us were deserving of God's good pleasure. It was His own delight that moved Him to bring us into His family. We should not be surprised that God chose some to salvation; we should be surprised that He chose any.

The old rug master sits on a stool somewhere in ancient Persia with his eyes closed. The aroma of wool fills the air. He can see the design in his mind. At his feet sit a row of young workers, each with a selection of wool strands, awaiting the master's commands.

He tells each of them what color to use next. They thread the strands and tie the knots, but they have little idea what design they are gradually creating. On their side of the rug the pattern seems confused and purposeless; but when the tapestry is finished and they get to look on the other side, they will stand amazed at its symmetry and beauty. Knot by knot the tapestry takes shape, though no one but the master can guess its pattern until the work is done. The workers must trust the master completely.

In a far greater way, God knows the pattern of the tapestry He is weaving in history. We are one of the threads, one of the pieces of wool. We are one little bit in God's great handiwork. The master's tapestry is a beautiful thing. By ourselves, we may not look like much. But when we get together, when we are as God saved us to be, holy and blameless, we make an absolutely impressive tapestry.

There are several ways in which the Book of Ephesians leads us to talk about patterns and tapestries. First, there is the emphasis on God's master plan for the universe. Second, there is the relational emphasis on God and His spiritual family, the

Church. Like any family, the family of God can be seen as a complex pattern of relationships throughout history and at any particular moment in history. The church is both an intricate tapestry and a dynamic family. This study seeks to highlight these wonderful lessons under the title *Life in God's Family.*

Before looking at this lesson's passage, let's step back for a moment and meet the Ephesians to whom the apostle Paul was writing. Ephesus was probably the second most important city in the Roman Empire. By today's standard, it represented an ideal pluralistic society—Ephesus was an "anything goes" city. Even now, the ruins of this great city bear silent witness to human creativity. Temples and magnificent public buildings have been ravaged by time but retain an aura of civic pride and achievement. Ephesus was a popular destination for religious tourists. The goddess Diana (Artemis) ruled over a crowd of other religions doing brisk business in the city.

Into this crowded religious marketplace came Paul with the Gospel of Jesus Christ. And his message created a stir. You see, Paul wasn't selling anything. He was offering something for free. In a place where the prevailing worldview put a price tag on everything from sex to spirituality, the Gospel brought the startling good news of hope that couldn't be bought for any price. The priceless treasure of God's grace could be received—*must* be received—freely by faith. So, it wasn't just the religious faith of the city that was in danger; it was the religious finances as well! (see Acts 19:1–41).

Paul began his letter to the Ephesians with the news that God's plan was designed from the start to include and benefit us. He described these benefits as spiritual blessings—all that Christ has obtained for His followers. These blessings *in* Christ include: 1) We are chosen to be holy and blameless (Eph. 1:4); 2) We are lovingly predestined for adoption in God's family (1:5); 3) We have redemption and forgiveness from sin (v. 7); 4) We have an eternal inheritance (v. 11); and 5) We have been sealed with the Holy Spirit (v. 13).

All of this is so amazing and undeserved that Paul calls it all "the mystery of his will, according to his purpose, which he set

> *"God knows the pattern of the tapestry He is weaving in history. We are one of the threads, one of the pieces of wool. We are one little bit in God's great handiwork."*

forth in Christ as a plan for the fullness of time" (vv. 9–10). God knows what He's doing. It's overwhelming to think that He's working out the design of His masterpiece tapestry in and through us! We don't just work on His tapestry; we *are* His tapestry!

One effective way to understand and remember the message of Ephesians is to realize that chapters 1–3 summarize all we have *in* Christ, and chapters 4–6 tell us how we can walk *with* Christ. The first half of the letter tells us who we are as God's family; the second half tells us how to live as God's family. And like an artist's sketch of a design or the way a composer weaves the musical themes of a symphony into the overture, the first fourteen verses of this letter give us a glimpse of Paul's entire message.

The order in the plan is crucial. You can't really experience what it means to walk *with* Christ until you understand what you have *in* Christ. Or to put it another way, every time you have difficulty walking with Christ you need to stop and remember what you have in Christ. Who you are and what you have in Christ motivates and makes possible what you do for Christ.

Express It

Before you pray, think for a few moments about what provokes awe in you about God's relationship with you. How do you respond to realizing that the One who created you wants to have fellowship and intimacy with you? Express to God how you feel about the privilege of being part of His family.

Consider It

As you read Ephesians 1:1–14, consider these questions:

1) What does Paul tell us about the Ephesians in this passage?

_____

_____

_____

2) How does each of the Persons in the Trinity (Father, Son and Holy Spirit) participate in God's plan (vv. 3–14)?

_____

_____

_____

3) What does it mean for Paul to "bless" God (v. 3)?

_____

_____

_____

4) Where does Paul include human responses in these verses?

_____

_____

_____

5) What does "redemption through his blood" mean (v. 7)?

_____

_____

_____

6) How does this passage describe God's choice of us?

_____

_____

_____

7) Why is sealing by the Holy Spirit an important part of God's plan?

_____

_____

_____

8) How is our "inheritance" (v. 11) both for now and for later?

_____

_____

_____

A Reason
for Prayer

We usually close our eyes for one of two reasons: to sleep or to pray. Unfortunately, though we aim for the latter (praying), we often end up doing the former (sleeping). Perhaps we should pray more with our eyes wide open. Or perhaps we should learn to pray like Paul prayed!

Ephesians 1:15–23

Thanksgiving and Prayer

[15]For this reason, because I have heard of your faith in the Lord Jesus and your love toward all the saints, [16]I do not cease to give thanks for you, remembering you in my prayers, [17]that the God of our Lord Jesus Christ, the Father of glory, may give you a spirit of wisdom and of revelation in the knowledge of him, [18]having the eyes of your hearts enlightened, that you may know what is the hope to which he has called you, what are the riches of his glorious inheritance in the saints, [19]and what is the immeasurable greatness of his power toward us who believe, according to the working of his great might [20]that he worked in Christ when he raised him from the dead and seated him at his right hand in the heavenly places, [21]far above all rule and authority and power and dominion, and

Key Verse

I do not cease to give thanks for you, remembering you in my prayers (Eph. 1:16).

above every name that is named, not only in this age but also in the one to come. [22]And he put all things under his feet and gave him as head over all things to the church, [23]which is his body, the fullness of him who fills all in all.

Go Deeper

A good habit Paul developed had to do with faith, hope and love. He could hardly think of one of these powerful pillars in our relationship with God without thinking of the other two. They are Paul's triumvirate of spiritual traits. In places like Romans 5:1–5, 1 Corinthians 13:1–13, Galatians 5:5–6 and Colossians 1:3–6, these three qualities work in harmony as part of God's plan. God is the giver and instigator of faith, hope and love. They are among His greatest gifts to us. In this lesson's passage (Ephesians 1:15–23), faith, hope and love play a crucial part in Paul's prayer for the Ephesians.

In a sense, Paul tells the Ephesians, "I've heard about the quality of your faith and love (v. 15), and that motivates me to pray for your hope (v. 18)." Paul's secretary must have struggled to keep up with the apostle's excitement. Phrases pile one on top of another. Those who exercise hope know they have a rich inheritance, and they also have confidence in God's power. Hope connects us with what God has waiting for us beyond this life. Hope reinforces our experience of faith and love every day. Develop the good habit of asking God to fill others with hope.

Bad habits are hard to break; good habits are hard to make. Almost any time we realize we've got a problem in our thinking, relating or acting, we can discover the root of the problem by asking, *What bad habit(s) have I picked up in this area?*

It's easy to develop a bad habit of immoral thought or just plain wrong thinking. Or we can slide into a bad habit of treating others with disrespect. Our internal habits always reveal themselves in our external behavior. One of the powerful applications of the last lesson fits here. If we get into the habit of ignoring whose we are and who we are in Christ, there are going to be negative results in the way we think, relate to others and behave. But a continual and humble acknowledgment of our undeserved privileges in God's family will lead to all kinds of good habits.

The apostle Paul had some good habits to teach us. He not only told the Ephesians that he prayed for them regularly, he also spelled out how he prayed for them. He wanted them to know the content of his prayers. He wanted them to be aware of ways in which God was answering his prayers for them. We can ask people to pray for us and even thank them for their prayers, but how often do we take time to describe how we experienced God answering their prayers on our behalf?

The missing link in this process is the "how." If we don't know how people are praying for us, it's difficult to tell them that God answered their prayers. Paul supplied the Ephesians with the "how." If fact, he did the same thing in almost every letter he wrote. (See, for example, Romans 1:8–10 and Philippians 1:3–11.) Imagine the depth of fellowship when he met with these believers and asked them, "So, you know how I've been praying for you. How has God been answering?"

Good habits need triggers. A trigger can be words or circumstances that act as reminders or "wake-up calls" for the habit. For Paul, receiving news was a trigger. He told the Ephesians, "For this reason, because I have heard of your faith in the Lord Jesus and your love toward all the saints" (Eph. 1:15). Paul was getting reports about the Ephesians, and he used them as a

> **"***If we make it a habit only to approach God with a list of requests but seldom enjoy His presence or get caught up in His majesty, then we are not experiencing prayer as God intended.***"**

reason to pray. Apparently, Paul would prepare to pray by asking, "Who am I thankful for today? What believers have encouraged me by their lives?" As those people came to mind, he remembered them in prayer (v. 16).

Now that's a great trigger! Instead of spending time wondering about his own standing with God, Paul *exercised* his position in Christ by identifying and thanking God for the good example and the very character of other believers. Similar to the concept of "it takes one to know one," Paul practiced the approach that "it takes one to pray for one"!

Among his requests to God on their behalf, Paul included a dual emphasis on "wisdom" and "revelation" (v. 17). He asked for God-given practicality. Then he asked God to grant the Ephesians a spiritual vision of hope—the capacity to see God's plan working out everywhere they looked, to savor the value of God's future rewards and to sense God's available power in the present moments.

God's power may be "immeasurable," but we begin to recognize its awesomeness by remembering it was the same power that raised Jesus from the dead. The very mention of this last item (God's power) acted as another habit trigger for Paul, releasing a flow of praise for Christ. We might call this Paul's good habit of doxology—he enjoyed composing expressions of appreciation for Christ and for God the Father's amazing plan.

Paul's pattern here illustrates a good habit and highlights one of our bad habits. We tend to approach praying for others like we handle shopping lists. The names are piled in a column in our minds and we go through them, ticking them off as we mention each one, frequently falling into a repetitive rhythm—"Bless Jane, bless Joe, bless Pete, and Lord, bless anyone else whose name I forgot!"

While this technically meets the definition of prayer, praying for someone ought to involve more than a brief mention of their name in God's presence. Maybe we still want to ask God to "bless" each of the people on our list, but we can personalize our prayer by speaking with God about how we see Him blessing them.

But Paul went beyond asking for blessings—all the way to letting his prayer times become continual expressions of fresh appreciation for God. If we make it a habit only to approach God with a list of requests but seldom enjoy His presence or get caught up in His majesty, then we are not experiencing prayer as God intended. We must make it a habit to spend the time it takes to sense we are in God's presence.

Express It

Before you pray, read Go Deeper. *Then re-read Ephesians 1:16–19, but substitute the name of someone for whom you have been praying in each place where Paul uses "you" or "your." As the Holy Spirit brings peoples' names to mind, make it a point to pray on their behalf for a fresh dose of hope.*

Consider It

As you read Ephesians 1:15–23, consider these questions:

1) How do you respond to good news about the lives of other Christians?

_____

_____

_____

2) How would you describe Paul's prayer attitude?

_____

_____

_____

3) What did Paul mean by the expression "eyes of your hearts" (v. 18)?

_____

_____

_____

4) How would you express Paul's prayer for the Ephesians in your own words?

_____

_____

_____

5) When you ask God for power, what kind of power are you asking for?

_____

_____

_____

_____

6) How would you respond if you knew someone was praying like this for you?

_____

_____

_____

_____

7) Who's on your prayer list right now, and how do you pray for them? Have you told them?

_____

_____

_____

_____

Where Faith Meets Grace

Can you imagine someone more helpless than a dead person? He can't do anything for himself or for anyone else. Paul reminds us that unless we realize we're dead, we will continuously make the mistake of thinking that we can help ourselves get to God.

Ephesians 2:1–10

By Grace Through Faith

2 And you were dead in the trespasses and sins [2]in which you once walked, following the course of this world, following the prince of the power of the air, the spirit that is now at work in the sons of disobedience—[3]among whom we all once lived in the passions of our flesh, carrying out the desires of the body and the mind, and were by nature children of wrath, like the rest of mankind. [4]But God, being rich in mercy, because of the great love with which he loved us, [5]even when we were dead in our trespasses, made us alive together with Christ—by grace you have been saved— [6]and raised us up with him and seated us with him in the heavenly places in Christ Jesus, [7]so that in the coming ages he might show the immeasurable riches of his grace in kindness toward us in Christ Jesus. [8]For by grace you have been saved through faith. And this is not your own doing; it is the gift of God, [9]not a result of works, so that no one may boast. [10]For we are his workmanship, created in Christ Jesus for good works, which God prepared beforehand, that we should walk in them.

Key Verse

For by grace you have been saved through faith. And this is not your own doing; it is the gift of God, not a result of works, so that no one may boast (Eph. 2:8–9).

Go Deeper

Do you want to go to heaven when you die? Most of us would say, "Yes." Do you know how to go to heaven when you die?

You don't go to heaven by the good things you do. The Bible clearly says our salvation is not obtained by works so we can boast about it. You can only get to heaven based on what God did for you.

What did God do for you? He asked Jesus to pay the penalty for your sin. He sent His Son to die at Calvary to atone for your sins. He made you spiritually alive. That's all done. If you have never personally responded before, this is your opportunity to exercise the faith God is giving you right now that only Jesus can save you from your sin.

Have you done that yet? Have you trusted Jesus as your Savior, or are you still living a life that is dead in trespasses and sins? If you've never trusted Jesus as Savior or if you're not sure, why don't you take a moment and let faith meet grace in your life? Tell Jesus you're accepting what He did to save you. Then start living a grateful life in the family of God!

The second chapter of Ephesians is actually the continuation of Paul's thought in the first chapter. He had just described God's power overcoming Jesus' death (Eph. 1:20) and confirming Jesus' place at the head of everything.

But all of this began when Paul was praying that the Ephesians would be filled with hope. And part of that hope was in God's power not only to manage the plan that revolved around Jesus but also to manage our predicament of sin.

In order to discuss that subject, Paul begins with a description of our condition: "dead in the trespasses and sins in which you once walked" (Eph. 2:1–2). Just as God had the will and the way to deal with Jesus' death, it follows that God has a will and a way to deal with our deadness in sin.

The first three verses of chapter 2 give us a realistic summary of the human condition. Though Paul starts with what reads like an accusation ("you once walked"), by the time he gets to the third verse everyone is included ("among whom we all once lived"). Deadness in sin is a universal human problem. The deadly virus has been passed to each generation at conception since our original human ancestors.

British author G. K. Chesterton was among a number of writers asked by the *London Times* to submit an essay on the question, "What's wrong with the world?" Chesterton sent in the clearest and most succinct reply: "Dear Sirs: I am. Sincerely yours, G. K. Chesterton." The apostle Paul would have said, "Me too." In Romans 3:23, Paul wrote, "For all have sinned and fall short of the glory of God."

The language of Ephesians 2 would provide an interesting title for a horror movie: *Life of the Walking Dead.* Part of the "tough love" message of the Gospel is this news that apart from Christ, we are spiritually dead. We may be fully functioning human beings, but we are spiritually lifeless. We can't talk ourselves, shock ourselves or work ourselves into spiritual life. We need spiritual intervention that only God can provide. The Bible frequently calls that intervention salvation, rescue or even deliv-

*"Apart from Christ we are spiritually dead. . . .
We can't talk ourselves, shock ourselves
or work ourselves into spiritual life.
We need spiritual intervention that only
God can provide."*

erance. (See Col. 1:13.) And we can't pay for it or earn it. God offers it free for the asking.

Ephesians 2:4–10 is an extended explanation to drive home the point that our salvation is God's business. Using the same power God used to raise Christ, God has raised believers and made us "alive" and "seated" with Him (vv. 5–6). Not only are we "with" Christ, we are "in" Christ (vv. 6–7). And in all of this, God's motive has been grace, His unmerited favor toward us.

But we should never quote Ephesians 2:8–9 without verse 10. They go together as a package. Verse 8 tells us *how* we are saved. Verse 9 tells us how we are *not* saved. Verse 10 tells us *why* we are saved. Salvation is the point at which faith meets grace. God's grace does the work; faith accepts the work. Both grace and faith ultimately are God's gifts, making the whole process God's.

We don't initiate any part of salvation. Our only involvement is receiving what God has done for us. No matter how humble our claim, as spiritually dead people, we simply cannot contribute anything to our own salvation. Jesus already did all the work for us on the cross.

Verse 10 then brings us to the purpose for our salvation. That word "workmanship" simply means His handiwork. The results of salvation have a lot to do with life in the family of God. He has saved us, and He is weaving us together as a living tapestry called

His Church. He is weaving us together as a beautiful treasure in the family of God.

We all have one thing in common. We were once dead fibers that have been raised with and by Jesus Christ. We have been created in Christ for good purposes—good works. The beautiful tapestry He calls His Church, the Master's tapestry, is the end result of being created in Christ. We are His handiwork. We are His family.

The good works God has prepared for us to walk in are before us as a result of salvation, not as a means to salvation. Our efforts to live a life that pleases our Heavenly Father flow from gratitude. He's already given us something we could never hope to earn. How could we not live our lives for Him?

Express It

God invites us to talk to Him. Prayer is always our R. S. V. P. And the crucial R. S. V. P. is when we use the gift of faith to receive the gift of grace that God offers (see Go Deeper). If you have already been "raised with Christ," ask Him for a fresh awareness of the good works God has prepared for you to do. Then ask Him for the willingness and strength to "walk in them."

Consider It

As you read Ephesians 2:1–10, consider these questions:

1) In what ways are all of us "dead in trespasses and sins" (v. 1)?

   _____

   _____

   _____

2) What does the word "walk" mean in verses 2 and 10?

   _____

   _____

   _____

3) What do these verses tell us about God's character?

   _____

   _____

   _____

4) How is salvation like being resurrected?

   _____

   _____

   _____

5) Beyond making us alive in Christ (v. 5), what else has God done for us?

   _____

   _____

   _____

6) At what point did faith meet grace in your life? What happened?

   _____

   _____

   _____

7) What happens if someone rejects the gift of grace and faith?

   _____

   _____

   _____

Who's in the Family?

God's family includes a mind-boggling assortment of unusual characters. To some extent, everyone has a checkered past. It's easy for us to wonder why He includes certain people "in the tapestry." But remember, people are probably wondering the same thing about us.

Ephesians 2:11–22

One in Christ

[11]Therefore remember that at one time you Gentiles in the flesh, called "the uncircumcision" by what is called the circumcision, which is made in the flesh by hands— [12]remember that you were at that time separated from Christ, alienated from the commonwealth of Israel and strangers to the covenants of promise, having no hope and without God in the world. [13]But now in Christ Jesus you who once were far off have been brought near by the blood of Christ. [14]For he himself is our peace, who has made us both one and has broken down in his flesh the dividing wall of hostility [15]by abolishing the law of commandments and ordinances, that he might create in himself one new man in place of the two, so making peace, [16]and might reconcile us both to God in one body through the cross, thereby killing the hostility. [17]And he came and preached peace to you who were far off and peace to those who were near. [18]For through him we both have access in one Spirit to the Father. [19]So then you are no longer strangers and aliens, but you are fellow citizens with the saints and members of the household of God, [20]built on the foundation of the apostles and prophets, Christ Jesus himself being the cornerstone, [21]in whom the whole structure, being joined together, grows into a holy temple in the Lord. [22]In him you also are being built together into a dwelling place for God by the Spirit.

Key Verse

So then you are no longer strangers and aliens, but you are fellow citizens with the saints and members of the household of God (Eph. 2:19).

Go Deeper

Notice the way Paul weaves "peace" throughout this passage. In verse 14, Christ "himself is our peace." His work in creating a brand-new kind of human being resulted in "peace" (v. 15). To those near and far, Jesus preached "peace" (v. 17). Paul's words reflect the message Jesus conveyed while on earth. "Peace I leave with you; my peace I give to you. Not as the world gives do I give to you. Let not your hearts be troubled, neither let them be afraid" (John 14:27).

When we are tempted to let our hearts be troubled, we need to let our hearts be at peace with Christ instead. Those were

Jesus' words after the Last Supper (John 14:27). Later, He added, "I have said these things to you, that in me you may have peace. In the world you will have tribulation. But take heart; I have overcome the world" (16:33).

Jesus didn't want us to expect from the world what the world can never deliver. But He did want us to look to Him for peace. Life in this world remains the same. The tribulation Jesus predicted for His disciples is just as true today as it was in the first century. But so is our source of peace. We can count on Him.

The apostle Paul believed in targeted remembering. He also believed in targeted forgetting. Certain past events we should never forget; others we should deliberately ignore. He told the Philippians, "But one thing I do: forgetting what lies behind and straining forward to what lies ahead, I press on toward the goal for the prize of the upward call of God in Christ Jesus" (Phil. 3:13–14).

Paul looked for believers who didn't let the past bog them down or trip them up. No matter what our history, we ought to be leaning forward and moving ahead in Christ. But Paul also wanted us to remember certain aspects of our past that can help us appreciate more fully what we have in the present and in the future. So, he issued a double-barreled reminder to remember in Ephesians 2:11–12. The encouragement to *remember* applies to this entire passage.

The Ephesian church was mainly composed of Gentiles (non-Jews). Acts 18:24–19:41 describes the early days of that congregation. Although Paul began his ministry in Ephesus with a three-month teaching series in the Jewish synagogue, strong resistance developed and he eventually moved into a public place. He taught Jewish and Gentile believers during the next two years. The very existence of that church was a tribute to God's power in Christ. "For he himself is our peace, who has made us both one and has broken down in his flesh the dividing wall of hostility" (Eph. 2:14).

That word "hostility" aptly describes the relationship that tends to exist any time one group sets itself apart from the rest of society. The Jews were a separate people. And nothing defined their "separateness" more than their devotion to a single God. In a world crowded with gods, anyone claiming not only to worship one God but also to be a people chosen by that one God was bound to provoke hostility from the surrounding community. The rest of the world has never quite gotten past its curiosity or hostility over the question of what makes the Jews so special.

This passage summarizes what Paul explained in much greater detail in the first 11 chapters of Romans. Paul didn't

> *"The peace that Jesus provides not only establishes a new relationship between any man or woman and Him, but it also establishes a kingdom of peace between people."*

teach that the Jews had lost their place in God's master plan even though they had rejected the Messiah. God knew what their response to the Messiah would be from the beginning and incorporated it into His plan.

What the Jews needed to learn was that at the heart of their role as the chosen people was a task to let all other people know that God had something special in mind for them too. Their separateness wasn't supposed to be a rejection of the rest of humanity but an invitation to know and worship the one true God with them. God chose them to be the people through whom He would come to earth and save the world.

By the time the Gospel arrived in Ephesus, a wall of deep hostility existed. Jewish spirituality had unraveled into proud cultural habits. Gentile spirituality was a hopeless mess of gross immorality masquerading as religion. "Remember that you were at that time separated from Christ, alienated from the commonwealth of Israel and strangers to the covenants of promise, having no hope and without God in the world" (2:12).

The expressions "separated," "alienated," "strangers," "having no hope" and "without God" are filled with despair. They describe not only the Ephesians, but also anyone who has not yet experienced salvation in Christ, the place where faith meets grace.

Paul's reason for pointing out the dividing wall was not to make the case that the Jews were on the right side and the Gentiles on the wrong side of the wall. The wall of separation represented a historic cultural and racial barrier. But those on both sides of the barrier needed Christ. The peace that Jesus provides not only establishes a new relationship between any man or woman and Him, but it also establishes a kingdom of peace between people, "by abolishing the law of commandments and ordinances, that he might create in himself one new man in place of the two, so making peace" (v. 15).

So, who's in the family? Paul gives us the good news. "Through him" (v. 18), Christ, all the barriers are removed and we are "fellow citizens with the saints and members of the household of God" (v. 19). Instead of a wall of separation, now there's a house of faith. In Christ, that house becomes a "temple in the Lord" (v. 21) and a "dwelling place for God by the Spirit" (v. 22). Jesus makes His home in us as individuals, and He also makes His home among us as He draws us together. In Christ, we are in God's family.

Express It

When Christians get along with each other, people notice. When Christians love one another, the world sits up and asks questions. If Jesus felt the need to pray that we would be one (John 17), we ought to follow His example and pray the same way. Ask God to make you aware of ways you can practice loving those with whom you might disagree about spiritual matters, not because they are particularly loveable but because you desire to obey Him.

Consider It

As you read Ephesians 2:11–22, consider these questions:

1) Apart from Christ, what is the spiritual condition of the Gentiles?

2) How did Jesus' death on the cross deal with our problem of separation?

3) What changed in the world because of Jesus' work on the cross?

4) Why did the "wall of separation" need to be demolished?

5) What replaced the "wall of separation"?

6) How does the Gospel break through social and religious barriers?

7) When and where have you most clearly experienced the oneness that Christians have in Christ despite any possible human obstacles?

8) What are your most treasured features of the new relationship that believers have in Christ?

A Message in the Mystery

Most of us want to pass through life leaving something more behind than a tombstone. We want our lives to stand for something. We want to leave some mark on the world. Paul discovered God had something in mind for him that would leave an impact greater than he could have ever dreamed up on his own.

Ephesians 3:1–13

The Mystery of the Gospel Revealed

3 For this reason I, Paul, a prisoner for Christ Jesus on behalf of you Gentiles— ²assuming that you have heard of the stewardship of God's grace that was given to me for you, ³how the mystery was made known to me by revelation, as I have written briefly. ⁴When you read this, you can perceive my insight into the mystery of Christ, ⁵which was not made known to the sons of men in other generations as it has now been revealed to his holy apostles and prophets by the Spirit. ⁶This mystery is that the Gentiles are fellow heirs, members of the same body, and partakers of the promise in Christ Jesus through the gospel.

⁷Of this gospel I was made a minister according to the gift of God's grace, which was given me by the working of his power. ⁸To me, though I am the very least of all the saints, this grace was given, to preach to the Gentiles the unsearchable riches of Christ, ⁹and to bring to light for everyone what is the plan of the mystery hidden for

> ## Key Verse
>
> *To me, though I am the very least of all the saints, this grace was given, to preach to the Gentiles the unsearchable riches of Christ* (Eph. 3:8).

ages in God who created all things, ¹⁰so that through the church the manifold wisdom of God might now be made known to the rulers and authorities in the heavenly places. ¹¹This was according to the eternal purpose that he has realized in Christ Jesus our Lord, ¹²in whom we have boldness and access with confidence through our faith in him. ¹³So I ask you not to lose heart over what I am suffering for you, which is your glory.

Go Deeper

"Mystery" does catch our attention and capture our imagination. But there are two common mistakes we make when we reflect on the word "mystery" as Paul uses it in Ephesians.

He uses the term seven times in Ephesians (1:9; 3:3,4,6,9; 5:32; 6:19). If we simply apply our external impressions of the word, we are likely to conclude that "mystery" refers to a puzzling circumstance that we can (like Sherlock Holmes) figure out, or that "mystery" refers to special secrets we may or may not be allowed to know. Neither of these fit Paul's meaning.

Paul isn't offering clues to a mystery so we can solve it; he's announcing the contents of the mystery—that access to God for both Jews and Gentiles is the same, through Jesus Christ. Nor is Paul engaging in the kind of "mystery religions" that were popular in his day (and are still around). These involved secret rites, codes and hidden knowledge accessible only to those "on the inside."

In contrast, the Gospel really is good news. The guesswork is removed. The mystery has been solved. God did what was necessary to let us know His love and grace. What's left of the mystery is the awe we feel at being included in God's grace and being the recipients of God's inexhaustible, "unsearchable" riches in Christ.

Paul had an impressive résumé. His background would have earned him a full page in the Jewish *Who's Who* of his time. His ministry for Christ made him one of the most in-demand people of the first century— some demanding his death, others hoping he would write or visit them with the Gospel.

Faced with all this good (and bad) popularity, Paul let us know he was painfully aware of the temptations that accompany being used by God. In 2 Corinthians 11 and 12, he described a heated argument over his credentials as an apostle. He reluctantly let his readers know the inside story of his calling, both the prestige and the persecutions he had received. He admitted he had a unique role but revealed that God had also given him a "thorn" to keep him humble. Paul never hesitated to point out, as he did to the Ephesians, that his job as God's spokesman was purely based on grace and not on any achievement of his own.

Paul never got over being an unexpected messenger who was privileged to proclaim God's unsearchable riches (Eph. 3:8). When he described his calling by God, Paul made sure people understood the joke was on him. He was a former fanatical hunter of the followers of Christ who, in turn, suddenly became the hunted. Jesus met him on the road to Damascus (Acts 9:1–19) and permanently altered his itinerary. God knocked him down to get his attention! In order for him to see clearly, God took away his sight. In order to give him a proper perspective, God sent Ananias, one of the Christians in Damascus on Paul's hit list, to pray for Paul so that his eyesight returned.

Paul's humility never undercut his message. His role as a servant didn't take away from the priceless value of his special duty as the apostle to the Gentiles. Like an insignificant messenger entrusted with a sealed scroll of state secrets, Paul pledged his life to safeguarding the "mystery" God had revealed to him.

So, what was this mystery? Paul also called it a message concerning the unsearchable riches of Christ. The Gospel is not an announcement that humans would have ever figured out without help. Despite all God's Old Testament clues, the world by and

> *"When it comes to the mystery of Christ, we can't know or figure out everything, but God has provided enough so that we can respond."*

large never saw God's grace in Jesus Christ coming. Those who were looking expected something or someone else. Jesus took earth by surprise. Not only did we not expect Jesus, we can never reach that place where we can confidently claim we have "figured Jesus out." His riches are unsearchable in the sense that they are beyond our full analysis. His grace and mercy are beyond our comprehension.

There's always more to discover about Jesus and the riches that are ours in Him. John was expressing this truth about Jesus when he wrote, "Now there are also many other things that Jesus did. Were every one of them to be written, I suppose that the world itself could not contain the books that would be written" (John 21:25). Paul summarizes the mystery in Ephesians 3:6: "This mystery is that the Gentiles are fellow heirs, members of the same body, and partakers of the promise in Christ Jesus through the gospel."

When it comes to the mystery of Christ, we can't know or figure out everything, but God has provided enough so that we can respond. One famous skeptic named Bertrand Russell is said to have remarked, "When I die, if it turns out there is a God who asks me why I didn't believe, I'll answer, 'You didn't give me enough information.'"

Sorry, Mr. Russell; that won't cut it. Then it will be too late. When we stand before the God revealed in Scripture, the last thing to cross our minds will be excuses, explanations or arguments. We will be face-to-face with Truth. In the meantime, God has given us more than enough reasons, facts and proofs upon which to base our trust. But He never gives us so much that faith is no longer required. We still have to respond personally. The mystery is that we actually get to respond!

It doesn't make sense to hold off the joy over being a fellow heir in Christ, having membership in His Body and owning part of God's promise in Jesus (Eph. 3:6) just because we can't explain it all. If we demand to have every question answered before we will accept God's grace, we will never accept it because God's grace is part of His "unsearchable" riches.

The testimony of countless believers through history has been that God allows us to understand enough of the message to believe, sometimes at a very early age. Once we trust, our understanding deepens. And the more we understand, the more the mystery of grace overwhelms us with wonder!

Express It

Paul closes this section with strong words of encouragement about Christ Jesus our Lord, "in whom we have boldness and access with confidence through our faith in him" (Eph. 3:12). What would it take for you to exercise boldness in prayer today? For whom would you pray? How would you pray? Prayer is not an arrogant presuming on God's favor any more than is a child's confident request of his or her loving father. Practice some childlike boldness in your prayer today.

Consider It

As you read Ephesians 3:1–13, consider these questions:

1) How does Paul describe his personal role in the spread of the Gospel in these verses?

To preach to Gentiles and to bring to light what is the administration of the mystery.

2) What phrases does Paul use here to define what he means by "mystery"?

3) Paul refers to "grace" in verses 2, 7 and 8. What is he describing?

4) Describe the role of the church (v. 10) in God's plan.

5) What experiences does Paul mention in verses 1 and 13 that he wants the Ephesians to take encouragement rather than discouragement from?

6) How do terms like "fellow heir," "members of the same body" and "partakers of the promise in Christ Jesus" (v. 6) affect you personally?

7) Why does Paul use the term "riches" (v. 8) to describe what Christ offers us?

A Life-Changing Prayer

Most memos end up in the circular file or are shredded. But you can probably remember some remarkable exceptions. That special note of encouragement or a supervisor's recognition of a service—those kinds of personal memos leave a lasting impression. But has anyone who prayed for you ever left a lasting mark?

Ephesians 3:14–21

Prayer for Spiritual Strength

¹⁴For this reason I bow my knees before the Father, ¹⁵from whom every family in heaven and on earth is named, ¹⁶that according to the riches of his glory he may grant you to be strengthened with power through his Spirit in your inner being, ¹⁷so that Christ may dwell in your hearts through faith—that you, being rooted and grounded in love, ¹⁸may have strength to comprehend with all the saints what is the breadth and length and height and depth, ¹⁹and to know the love of Christ that surpasses knowledge, that you may be filled with all the fullness of God.

²⁰Now to him who is able to do far more abundantly than all that we ask or think, according to the power at work within us,

Key Verse

So that Christ may dwell in your hearts through faith— that you, being rooted and grounded in love (Eph. 3:17).

²¹to him be glory in the church and in Christ Jesus throughout all generations, forever and ever. Amen.

Go Deeper

Paul sets up his prayer for the Ephesians by stating his core motivation. Ephesians 3:14 is the second time in this chapter that he has used the phrase, "For this reason." He began the chapter with the same phrase (v. 1). Since the force of "this" indicates that Paul is thinking of what immediately precedes, we can see that a powerful idea drove Paul to preach and to pray.

To understand the "reason" for Paul's actions, we can look at Ephesians 2:21–22 and 3:11–13. The subject of both these passages is Jesus Christ and His eternal, central role in God's plan. Notice the phrases: "in whom" (2:21), "in the Lord" (2:21), "in him" (2:22), "in Christ Jesus" (3:11), "in whom" (3:12) and "in him" (3:12). The faith we share

begins with Jesus Christ, remains rooted in Him and comes back to Him.

Whether Paul was thinking about his present situation as a prisoner in a cell or his privilege to encourage the Ephesian believers, he realized everything revolved around Christ. Neither Jew nor Gentile could access God apart from Christ. For that reason, why not live in Christ? Why not bow before God and claim Christ's indwelling, Spirit-empowered, love-immersed life? That was certainly a good enough reason for Paul. It ought to be a good enough reason for us!

How often does someone pray for you by name? What would be your response if you listened in on a prayer by someone whose words to God revealed exactly what you longed to experience but had a hard time putting into your own words?

That's the kind of prayer Paul expresses for the Ephesians in these verses. And this prayer applies just as clearly and as powerfully today and to your life as the day Paul first penned it for the Ephesians. It's a prayer we can still use in the church to pray for one another by name.

This prayer serves as a wonderful transition in Paul's letter between the weighty teaching of the first three chapters and the challenging practical applications found in the last three chapters. If we view the first three chapters as the mystery of grace, we can think of the last three chapters as the mechanics of grace. The first three chapters are about all that God has done; the last three are about all that we can do in response. Paul began by telling us who we are and what we have in Christ. Now he's preparing to tell us what we can become in Christ. So, this prayer concludes the instruction section with a benediction of inspiration.

To begin with, it's worth noting that Paul spent little time explaining the Trinity and much of his time praying to God, the Three-in-One. Throughout his writings, he naturally reports his interaction with God the Father, God the Son and God the Holy Spirit. His background as a highly trained Jewish monotheist (strict believer in one God) makes his intimacy with the Trinity an attitude we ought to copy. God as Three-in-One remains impossible to fully explain, but the difficulties fade when we begin to simply address God as Three-in-One.

Paul tells us in this passage that he bows to the Father (Eph. 3:14), anticipates the Spirit's empowering (3:16), and asks for Christ's indwelling (v. 17) as he prays. Paul expects that the result of his prayer will be a powerful experience of the "fullness of God" (v. 19). Then he closes with a doxology to Him who is at one and the same time the Father who "is able to do far more abundantly than all that we ask or think" (v. 20), the Holy Spirit powerfully "at

> *"If our root system is growing down into Christ's love, we will never become root-bound. The soil of God's love is inexhaustible in every direction: breadth, length, height and depth."*

work within us" (v. 20) and Christ Jesus (v. 21) who reflects in human form the full glory of God. We would do well to fix our minds on this awesome God before whom we bow in prayer.

This prayer of Paul's is one of the rare times in his letters when he mentions faith and love without specifically including hope. Since the entire prayer is permeated by hope, Paul manages to include the believer's hope even when he doesn't use the word. Here we see the intimate work of God's Spirit strengthening us for Christ's indwelling "through faith" (v. 17).

This phrase sends us back to Jesus' own words in John 15:4–5: "Abide in me, and I in you. As the branch cannot bear fruit by itself, unless it abides in the vine, neither can you, unless you abide in me. I am the vine; you are the branches. Whoever abides in me and I in him, he it is that bears much fruit, for apart from me you can do nothing."

Our relationship with Jesus is like no other. He abides (or dwells) in us, and we abide in Him. Or, to use the picture Paul paints with words here, He dwells in us and our roots grow down into His love.

People who grow ornamental bushes for indoor use know that plants need to be re-potted from time to time in order to stay healthy. As a bush grows, its roots gradually fill all the space in a pot. If a larger container of soil isn't provided, the plant will become unhealthy or die. God's Word often pictures us as plants and trees for various purposes. Our dependence on God's Word makes us like trees "planted by streams of water" (Ps. 1:3). If our root system is growing down into Christ's love, we will never become root-bound. The soil of God's love is inexhaustible in every direction: breadth, length, height and depth (Eph. 3:18). God's love is so vast that we need "strength to comprehend" it (3:18). This doesn't mean we comprehend by measuring the dimensions of God's love but by realizing that we can't reach the ends of it!

How can you "know" something that "surpasses knowledge" (v. 19)? Knowing can be real without being complete. This is always true in relationships. You know each other more and more, but you can never know each other completely. (Complete knowledge is left to God alone.) But the privilege of knowing Christ is wonderful and a worthy request you should always ask God to provide in greater and greater measure to yourself and all those in your life.

Express It

Identify several individuals or groups that hold a special place in your life. Use this prayer of Paul's as a model and intentionally pray for those individuals or groups over the next week. Keep track of your internal and external observations as you undertake this prayer project.

Consider It

As you read Ephesians 3:14–21, consider these questions:

1) What observations can you make about Paul's prayer life based on this passage?

_____

_____

_____

2) Both verses 3:1 and 3:14 begin, "For this reason." To what reason is Paul referring?

_____

_____

_____

3) How would you describe the height, length, depth and breadth of God's love?

_____

_____

_____

4) What does it mean to have Christ dwell in you by faith?

_____

_____

_____

5) Through what means have you become more firmly rooted in Christ's love?

_____

_____

_____

6) How would you summarize Paul's prayer in one sentence?

_____

_____

_____

7) Explain Paul's doxology (vv. 20–21) in your own words.

_____

_____

_____

A Life Tour

"That's it, folks! Everyone back on the bus." Visits to exotic places often involve large groups of travelers. Tours merge strangers for economical and "worry-free" travel. But tours have their own stress points, like imposed schedules, cross purposes and clashing personalities. The Body of Christ is the world's largest touring group. No wonder the journey presents a few challenges as well as surprises!

Ephesians 4:1–16

Unity in the Body of Christ

4 I therefore, a prisoner for the Lord, urge you to walk in a manner worthy of the calling to which you have been called, ²with all humility and gentleness, with patience, bearing with one another in love, ³eager to maintain the unity of the Spirit in the bond of peace. ⁴There is one body and one Spirit—just as you were called to the one hope that belongs to your call— ⁵one Lord, one faith, one baptism, ⁶one God and Father of all, who is over all and through all and in all. ⁷But grace was given to each one of us according to the measure of Christ's gift. ⁸Therefore it says,

> "When he ascended on high he led a host of captives,
>
> and he gave gifts to men."

⁹(In saying, "He ascended," what does it mean but that he had also descended into the lower parts of the earth? ¹⁰He who descended is the one who also ascended far above all the heavens, that he might fill all things.) ¹¹And he gave the apostles, the prophets, the evangelists, the pastors and teachers, ¹²to equip the saints for the work of ministry, for building up the body of Christ, ¹³until we all attain to the unity of the faith and of the knowledge of the Son of God, to mature manhood, to the measure of the stature of the fullness of Christ, ¹⁴so that we may no longer be children, tossed to and fro by the waves and carried about by every wind of doctrine, by human cunning, by craftiness in deceitful schemes. ¹⁵Rather, speaking the truth in love, we are to grow up in every way into him who is the head, into Christ, ¹⁶from whom the whole body, joined and held together by every joint with which it is equipped, when each part is working properly, makes the body grow so that it builds itself up in love.

Key Verse

I therefore, a prisoner for the Lord, urge you to walk in a manner worthy of the calling to which you have been called (Eph. 4:1).

Go Deeper

The world is watching to see whether we get along with other believers. What do they see? Those of us who come from every tribe and nation, those of us who are drawn from both Jews and Gentiles, those of us who are one in Christ sometimes don't walk like we're one in Christ, do we? When we don't, we're not walking worthy of the Lord.

Ephesians 4:4–6 is a striking passage on the unity of the Body of Christ. Note how many times the word "one" is used. In verse 4, the key character is the Spirit of God. The Holy Spirit creates the Body and fills it with peace and hope. In verse 5, the key character is the Lord Jesus Christ. He is Lord of the Church and anchor point of our faith. Into His name

(continued)

Go Deeper Continued . . .

we are baptized. In verse 6, the key character is God the Father Himself. He is everywhere, to everyone and in every way present within the Body of Christ. Our unity as believers ought to reflect the unity in the Trinity. That desire for unity ought to be the background tune of our lives and the underlying theme of our prayers.

With the opening words of Ephesians 4, Paul makes a transition. He shifts from doctrine to practice. There will still be some doctrine in the chapters yet to come, but most of Ephesians 4–6 is simply applying the thought of unity—that Jesus died both for Jews and for Gentiles, that before the foundation of the world God planned and preordained salvation and that salvation was not just of the Jewish people. It was the salvation of mankind. It was the salvation of people out of every tribe and nation. It was your salvation and my salvation.

That news reaches each of us like a voice calling into our lives. If we believe that call is true and accept it, we must take seriously the challenge to "walk in a manner worthy of the calling" (Eph. 4:1).

Given that challenge, Paul begins to describe how salvation works out in daily living. How do we put into practice what God has already foreordained should be the case, that we get along with one another in the church? Unity. We walk in a worthy manner when we walk in unity—not the external or organizational kind, but the internal, organic kind of unity.

This is not a unity that is superimposed upon the church. It's a unity that rises from within, because we all have the same Savior and Lord living within. Walking worthy means we get along. We work together in the cause of Christ. We can only do that when we recognize that we bring nothing to this unity. Everything we have, every gift we use, everything we are depends entirely upon the grace of God.

A great former manager of the New York Yankees once said, "It's easy to get good players. Getting them to play together, now that's the hard part." In the church, it's easy to get good people. But getting good people to work together, now that's the hard part. Fortunately, God's Word describes the process God will use to make visible what He already sees in the Body of Christ.

The Church is spiritually one, and as a result, every believer in the Church is to make an effort to preserve that spiritual unity. That's what we see in the first several verses of Ephesians 4. But just because we're unified does not mean that we lose all our individuality. In fact, in verses 7–12, Paul shows us that individual expression is very much encouraged. Unity can include diversity; in fact, unity demands diversity. The unity that we have in Jesus Christ is a unity of purpose. Our purpose is to be a blessing to one another. Our purpose is to walk worthy of the Lord so that we can build up the Church, so that we as a Church can be a blessing to the world. Our unity will come when we learn how to walk together.

We walk worthy of the Lord in these five ways. Look at them in Ephesians 4:2–3: 1) with all humility, 2) gentleness, 3) patience, 4) bearing with one another in love, and 5) eager to maintain the unity of the Spirit in the bond of peace. As you review these, note that every one of them is developed in community. We require each other in order to walk worthy of the Lord.

A worthy life begins with humility. Receiving the blessings of salvation, the blessings of being called into one Body, the blessings of being a part of God's wonderful tapestry—ought to bring us to an attitude of humility. Humility has been called the first, the second and the third essential of the Christian life. You walk worthy when you walk humbly before the Lord. Gentleness (or meekness) is another part of walking worthy. A meek individual is one who never insists upon his own rights. We do have rights as believers. But if we read 1 Corinthians 6, we discover that it is sometimes better not to exercise those rights, even though we have them, so we can walk worthy of the Lord.

The third way to walk worthy of Christ's call involves patience (or longsuffering). Essentially, patience means that when someone is having a problem, we are willing to go the extra mile with him or her. We're willing to "long suffer" with that person. We're not

"The unity that we have in Jesus Christ is a unity of purpose. Our purpose is to be a blessing to one another. Our purpose is to walk worthy of the Lord so that we can build up the Church, so that we as a Church can be a blessing to the world."

going to cut them off just because they fall. We will pick them up and help them again and again. That's patience. That's walking worthy of the vocation for which you and I are called.

The words "bearing with one another in love" act like the fraternal twin of patience. If longsuffering is our response to others, then "bearing with" is our response to their treatment of us. When others hurt or misunderstand us, we do not react in kind. We "put up" with it for Christ's sake. That's also a part of walking worthy.

Finally, Paul says walking worthy is eagerness to keep the unity of the Spirit. We are sensitive to the Spirit's urges to maintain unity despite the pressure to splinter that the world, the flesh and the devil exert on us.

Express It

With the words of Ephesians 4:1–6 in mind, read John 17 prayerfully, out loud. Think of Jesus' prayer as His prayer for you. Borrow as much of that prayer as possible as you pray for the Church at large and your church in particular. Try to imagine what it would mean to experience a greater degree of unity with the believers you know. Ask God for His guidance in your role within the Body of Christ as someone who wants to cooperate in making the actual unity of Christ's Church more visible in the world.

Consider It

As you read Ephesians 4:1–16, consider these questions:

1) On what occasions have you most clearly experienced the true effects of people "walking worthy of their calling"?

2) Rank the five unity-reinforcing qualities that Paul lists in verses 2–3 (humility, gentleness, patience, love and peacemaking) according to your present level of spiritual development.

3) What is it about the local church of which you're a part that makes it a good training ground for your character development?

4) How do you (intentionally or unintentionally) contribute to the development of others?

5) In what ways do the seven "ones" Paul lists in verses 4–6 define for you what it means to be an authentic follower of Jesus Christ?

6) What is the role of the special assignments God gives in verse 11?

7) How do verses 7–16 describe the part every believer is to carry out as a member of Christ's Body?

Lesson

8

Spiritual Conditioning

For most of us, the goal of physical exercise has more to do with conditioning than the development of unusual strength or massive muscles. We'd gladly settle for firmness over bulk! How can we compare physical fitness with spiritual fitness? What does it mean to be in good spiritual health, and how do we get there?

Ephesians 4:17–32

The New Life

¹⁷Now this I say and testify in the Lord, that you must no longer walk as the Gentiles do, in the futility of their minds. ¹⁸They are darkened in their understanding, alienated from the life of God because of the ignorance that is in them, due to their hardness of heart. ¹⁹They have become callous and have given themselves up to sensuality, greedy to practice every kind of impurity. ²⁰But that is not the way you learned Christ!— ²¹assuming that you have heard about him and were taught in him, as the truth is in Jesus, ²²to put off your old self, which belongs to your former manner of life and is corrupt through deceitful desires, ²³and to be renewed in the spirit of your minds, ²⁴and to put on the new self, created after the likeness of God in true righteousness and holiness.

²⁵Therefore, having put away falsehood, let each one of you speak the truth with his neighbor, for we are members one of another. ²⁶Be angry and do not sin; do not let the sun go down on your anger, ²⁷and give no opportunity to

> # Key Verse
>
> *But that is not the way you learned Christ!* (Eph. 4:20).

the devil. ²⁸Let the thief no longer steal, but rather let him labor, doing honest work with his own hands, so that he may have something to share with anyone in need. ²⁹Let no corrupting talk come out of your mouths, but only such as is good for building up, as fits the occasion, that it may give grace to those who hear. ³⁰And do not grieve the Holy Spirit of God, by whom you were sealed for the day of redemption. ³¹Let all bitterness and wrath and anger and clamor and slander be put away from you, along with all malice. ³²Be kind to one another, tenderhearted, forgiving one another, as God in Christ forgave you.

Go Deeper

Beyond the two examples provided in this lesson's main study, Paul included an application of his training regimen on three other character traits ripe for change in many of us: work ethics (Eph. 4:28), verbal control (4:29–30) and relational impact (vv. 31–32). The principle of going deeper for this lesson doesn't refer to more insight but to greater intentional application of the meaning of "walking (living) worthy" of Christ's calling in our lives.

When it comes to theft of any kind, Paul instructs us to reject any action that takes what isn't ours. Instead, we should understand that the purpose of stewardship isn't

hoarding but helping others. We are to do honest work and share what we earn. Likewise, we should discard that old outfit of outrageous words we may have been "wearing." Learning Christ means becoming keenly aware that our language "corrupts" others and grieves the Holy Spirit. Instead we are to help others be "built up" by our words.

Finally, we are to refrain from any negative actions and attitudes that hurt and push people away. Learning Christ involves a deeper and deeper realization of all we have been forgiven by God in Christ and forgiving others as a result.

Too many of us are "Someday Athletes." Our thoughts and plans about exercise always begin with "someday." Someday, I'll get a membership at the gym. Someday, I'm going to start getting in shape. Someday, I'm going to actually get on the _____ (fill in the appropriate exercise machine: stationary bike, treadmill, stepper, etc.) that I bought at Christmas two years ago and still haven't taken out of the box!

Lots of Christians live their lives as "Someday Spiritual Athletes." Someday we'll get serious about prayer. Someday we'll read through the Bible. Someday we will start a regular habit of daily time with God. Someday we'll have a consistent relationship with a local church.

If there's one thing we know about "somedays," it's that "somedays" never come. Have you ever gotten out of bed in the morning, stretched and then exclaimed, "Oh, today is someday! I've got lots to do"? We had yesterday, we have today and, the Lord willing, we will have tomorrow. God gives "todays," not "somedays."

One of the most sober challenges in all of Scripture was penned by the apostle Paul to the Corinthians: "Behold, now is the favorable time; behold, now is the day of salvation" (2 Cor. 6:2). What would happen if every time we realized we just said, "Someday," we backed up and said, "No, *today* I'm going to _____," and then we did it?

Among the healthiest of exercises is walking. It accomplishes a lot of good with minimal stress (compared to running, which has more cardiovascular benefits but can be hard on our bones). In the Bible, walking represents living. Twice in Ephesians 4, Paul uses the word "walk" to write about two very different lives: the Christian life (4:1) and the futile life (v. 17). Those of us who claim to "follow" Jesus Christ can't stand still—we are called to walk!

Fortunately, Paul helps us know how to apply the principle of spiritual walking to each day of life. As is true of physical walking, our progress may not seem remarkable, but it will be real.

> *"We had yesterday, we have today and, the Lord willing, we will have tomorrow. God gives "todays," not "somedays."*

The key verse for this passage is, "But that is not the way you learned Christ!" (v. 20). This declaration forms a bridge between Paul's description of the "ordinary, unbelieving (futile) life" and the life God intends us to live. So, how *did* we learn Christ?

Paul explains that learning Christ involves both the place you start and the process of continuing what was started. You begin learning Christ the day you come to Him in faith. That's the day you "put off your old self" (v. 22) and "put on the new self" (v. 24). That simply means you are no longer the old person you were in your sins. You were born into the family of Adam. Unfortunately, that also means you were born a sinner and condemned to death as a result (Rom. 3:23; 6:23). But when you trusted Christ as your Savior, you were born again, this time into the family of Christ. You became a new creation in Christ Jesus (2 Cor. 5:17). That's where learning Christ begins, but it's not where it ends.

Each day "in Christ" is an adventure, an adventure in "learning Christ." It's a training exercise moving down the road toward the goal of really knowing Christ. (See Phil. 3:10.)

In the remainder of this chapter (Eph. 4:25–32), Paul provides five brief case studies illustrating how this training exercise helps us get in shape spiritually. The five cases involve the areas of honesty (4:25), anger management (vv. 26–27), work ethics (v. 28), verbal control (vv. 29–30) and relational impact (vv. 31–32).

When it comes to honesty, you must "put away falsehood" (v. 25). Instead of giving in to easy lying, ask God for a "hunger and thirst for righteousness" (Matt. 5:6). You learn Christ by gaining a sense of connection with other believers, "for we are members one of another" (Eph. 4:25). As a result, you decide only to speak the truth (4:25) to those around you.

You can "be angry," but you have to deal with it before it becomes sin and before you go to bed. Learning Christ means realizing that mismanaged anger gives an "opportunity to the devil" (v. 27). It also means expressing anger in healthy and short-term ways. The habit of holding anger overnight has deadly and sinful consequences. It leaves the door open for sin all night and has settled in by morning. Close the door on sin before you close your eyes in sleep.

As you trace the other three training exercises (see *Go Deeper*), rejoice that as a new person in Christ you can learn to live His way. He has a full life, not a futile life, in mind for you!

Express It

Ask God to help you identify areas where you are spiritually "out of shape." Make a list of them. Acknowledge you have been putting off dealing with them until "someday." Now ask God to lift them off you and begin the process of renewal and restoration in your life. Give God's Spirit full permission to pester you until you take some action in these areas today.

Consider It

As you read Ephesians 4:17–32, consider these questions:

1) According to Paul, what goes into creating a futile life?

2) How does Paul challenge his readers not to assume they have learned Christ (v. 21)?

3) What do you think most about when you set out to identify your "old self"?

4) What are the primary characteristics of the "new self" Paul describes in v. 24?

5) As you read through those five "case studies," which one(s) touched a nerve in your life?

6) Based on this passage, what will you do about that issue today?

7) In what areas have you struggled the most with being a "someday" Christian?

More Walking

In the last two lessons, Paul introduced us to different phases of spiritual walking. First we learned to walk in a worthy manner. Then we learned to stop walking in futility and start walking with usefulness and purpose. In this lesson, we get another look at the way God expects us to walk (live).

Ephesians 5:1–21

Walk in Love

5 Therefore be imitators of God, as beloved children. ²And walk in love, as Christ loved us and gave himself up for us, a fragrant offering and sacrifice to God.

³But sexual immorality and all impurity or covetousness must not even be named among you, as is proper among saints. ⁴Let there be no filthiness nor foolish talk nor crude joking, which are out of place, but instead let there be thanksgiving. ⁵For you may be sure of this, that everyone who is sexually immoral or impure, or who is covetous (that is, an idolater), has no inheritance in the kingdom of Christ and God. ⁶Let no one deceive you with empty words, for because of these things the wrath of God comes upon the sons of disobedience. ⁷Therefore do not associate with them; ⁸for at one time you were darkness, but now you are light in the Lord. Walk as children of light ⁹(for the fruit of light is found in all that is good and right and true), ¹⁰and try to discern what is pleasing to the Lord. ¹¹Take no part in the unfruitful works of darkness, but instead expose them. ¹²For it is shameful even to speak of the things that they do in secret. ¹³But when anything is exposed by the light, it becomes visible, ¹⁴for anything that becomes visible is light. Therefore it says,

> *Key Verse*
>
> And walk in love, as Christ loved us and gave himself up for us, a fragrant offering and sacrifice to God (Eph. 5:2).

"Awake, O sleeper,

and arise from the dead,

and Christ will shine on you."

¹⁵Look carefully then how you walk, not as unwise but as wise, ¹⁶making the best use of the time, because the days are evil. ¹⁷Therefore do not be foolish, but understand what the will of the Lord is. ¹⁸And do not get drunk with wine, for that is debauchery, but be filled with the Spirit, ¹⁹addressing one another in psalms and hymns and spiritual songs, singing and making melody to the Lord with all your heart, ²⁰giving thanks always and for everything to God the Father in the name of our Lord Jesus Christ, ²¹submitting to one another out of reverence for Christ.

Go Deeper

Do you know what it means to walk carefully (Eph. 5:15)? One of the significant dangers for people in Bosnia today is the over two million land mines planted in their country during the war a decade ago. These land mines go off from the pressure of anyone stepping on them—men, women or children. You and

I need to walk in such a way that we do not step on spiritual land mines. Satan's strategy is to lay land mines in our lives. Sin doesn't just trip us; sometimes it blows up in our faces. That's why Paul says we need to walk carefully. We need to watch where we put our feet down.

(continued)

Go Deeper Continued . . .

The word for "carefully" in Greek is the word that means "to walk exactly and accurately." We walk wide-awake. When we live deliberately, we're not walking as foolish people. How do foolish people walk? The Bible has a lot to say to contrast the way fools and the wise conduct their lives. See, for example, Proverbs 3:35, 11:29, 12:15, 13:20, 14:9.

Notice the connection between Proverbs 1:2–7 about walking worthy of the Lord and walking in wisdom. If we walk in a way that pleases God, we will walk in a way that displeases the foolish people around us. If we want God's eternal approval, we may have to live with earthly disapproval in a lot of areas. Wise people are those who live by God's Word.

Children are born imitators. Daddy's shoes may not fit the little boy and Mom's hat may cover half her daughter's face, but pretending to be parents is part of the informal training of childhood. We imitate roles until we get to live them. Ephesians 5 firmly puts us among God's family and tells us that as children we ought to be "imitators of God" (5:1). But being an imitator of God is a tall order.

Have you ever wondered how you can be an imitator of God? The first step would be to know the God you are seeking to imitate. The Lord says, "Be still, and know that I am God" (Ps. 46:10). Sometimes, no matter how still we try to be, we just can't seem to know God the way we want to. We may want to imitate Him, but we can't even fathom that possibility. We end up feeling like children who want to play dress-up but can't find anything our Heavenly Father would wear. How do we imitate an invisible person?

Fortunately, God doesn't ask us to do things He's not willing to help us accomplish. Knowing our helplessness, He chose to become someone we could imitate—Jesus Christ. God wore a human body so we *could* see what it's like for God to live at our level. Colossians 1:19 tells us, "For in him all the fullness of God was pleased to dwell." We don't dress up in God's clothes; we dress up in God's Son.

Now there are important differences between imitating Jesus and trying to duplicate what He did. We are called to imitate, not duplicate. What Jesus did as our perfect sacrifice for sins only had to be done and only could be done one time. Hebrews tells us He died "once for all when he offered up himself" (Heb. 7:27).

Jesus requires but one standard in the way that we love. He asks not that our love equal His, but *resemble* His. We can't love exactly the way Jesus loved. Jesus loved us so much that He died for us. He went to the cross and sacrificed His life for us. We can't love entirely that way, but we can use that love as a model. That's why Paul essentially says in Ephesians 5:2, "If you want to be a follower of God, if you want to imitate God, you have to do it the way Jesus did." Here's how Jesus did it: He walked in love.

Like little children, we watch intently what Jesus did and said and then follow in His footsteps. We treat Jesus as our mentor and our model. God's Word gives us vivid glimpses of Jesus in action—getting up from the table and wrapping a servant's towel around His waist and then washing the feet of the disciples. We're told in John 13 that He did that to show His love. Then He told His disciples to love one another the way He had just demonstrated.

Stop for a moment, and look at the parallels. Who can we serve? We may have to get up from the table and wash the dishes without being asked. We may have to clear snow from the walk of the elderly widow next door. When we practice small voluntary, sacrificial actions for others, we gain a deeper appreciation of the depth of Jesus' sacrifice for us. How can we claim to understand what Jesus did and why He did it if His actions on our behalf don't drive us to serve others?

Ephesians 5:3–14 almost seems out of place until we realize that we often begin to walk in love by ceasing to walk the way the world walks. The behaviors Paul mentions in these verses are often the first ones where Christians compromise. The world whispers and shouts to us about self-centered living/walking. Paul describes those who walk in darkness and calls us to "walk as children of light" (Eph. 5:8).

"God doesn't ask us to do things He's not willing to help us accomplish. Knowing our helplessness, He chose to become someone we could imitate—Jesus Christ."

Walking in love as Jesus walked doesn't come naturally. If we live by our feelings and wisdom, we will live like the world. That's why Paul reminds us that we need to give attention to how we walk/live. "Look carefully then how you walk, not as unwise but as wise" (5:15). We must intentionally decide to walk in love and depend on Christ to bring that quality in increasing amounts into our lives.

Neither wisdom nor love grows accidentally. Both require that we devote ourselves to "making the best use of time, because the days are evil" (v. 16). Wisdom and love grow as we deliberately seek them in Christ.

Express It

Meditate on the significance of a prayer by David the king: "Your word is a lamp to my feet and a light to my path" (Ps. 119:105). Tell God about some of the ways you appreciate the role His Word plays in your life.

Consider It

As you read Ephesians 5:1–21, consider these questions:

1) How do you picture yourself imitating God?

2) What specific attitudes and actions did Paul warn the Ephesians about?

3) In what ways do Paul's warnings still apply today?

4) What does it mean to "discern what is pleasing to the Lord" (v. 10)?

5) How does Paul use "light" and "darkness" in this passage?

6) What does making the "best use of time" have to do with "the days are evil" (v. 16)?

7) In what areas are you experiencing what it means to be filled with the Holy Spirit?

8) How well are you interacting with others in God's family as fellow beloved children?

Tough Roles

No doubt about it, the word "submit" is on the world's hit list. Bring it up in a discussion on marriage, and resistance will rise like the hair on the back of your neck. But, with the word submission in mind, this lesson allows us to consider which partner in a marriage has the toughest, most challenging role: husband or wife.

Ephesians 5:22–33

Wives and Husbands

22Wives, submit to your own husbands, as to the Lord. 23For the husband is the head of the wife even as Christ is the head of the church, his body, and is himself its Savior. 24Now as the church submits to Christ, so also wives should submit in everything to their husbands.

25Husbands, love your wives, as Christ loved the church and gave himself up for her, 26that he might sanctify her, having cleansed her by the washing of water with the word, 27so that he might present the church to himself in splendor, without spot or wrinkle or any such thing, that she might be holy and without blemish. 28In the same way husbands should love their wives as their own bodies. He who loves his wife loves himself. 29For no one ever hated his own flesh, but nourishes and cherishes it, just as Christ does the church,

> # Key Verse
>
> *However, let each one of you love his wife as himself, and let the wife see that she respects her husband* (Eph. 5:33).

30because we are members of his body. 31"Therefore a man shall leave his father and mother and hold fast to his wife, and the two shall become one flesh." 32This mystery is profound, and I am saying that it refers to Christ and the church. 33However, let each one of you love his wife as himself, and let the wife see that she respects her husband.

Go Deeper

There are very good reasons for men to love their wives the way Jesus loved the Church. Some are found in Ephesians 5:26–27. The purpose for which a man loves his wife is not so she will be submissive to him. Rather, that purpose is exactly the same purpose for which Jesus loved the Church. It is a man's responsibility as the head of the home and as a loving husband to do whatever is necessary both positively and negatively to see that his wife is an absolutely cleansed and sanctified vessel for the Lord.

When Paul writes that Jesus gave Himself and loved the Church that He might sanctify and cleanse her, he is saying that this twofold process—sanctifying

and cleansing—is necessary, and it's never finished until death. One of the things that a husband ought to bring to a marriage is the kind of godliness that enables him to set apart his wife for the Lord God, to sanctify her and to wash her—to assist in the process of daily confessing sin, daily getting close to the Lord, daily making sure that we keep short accounts with God (see also Titus 2:5, 1 Pet. 3:7).

If you're really the man in your house, you'll be a spiritual giant to your wife. You'll be the leader of your home. You'll be the spiritual head of your house, not just the one who barks orders around. You'll practice love.

All the participants and the parts are in place. Lovely flowers, flickering candles and the festive colors of a wedding ceremony have created an impressive visual palate. The groom's men stand stiffly at attention. Bridesmaids turn center stage and smile in anticipation of their future prospects or with memories of their own wedding. Bride and groom look into each other's eyes trying to focus on the significance of the moment. They barely hear the minister reading the words to Ephesians 5:22–33. When he's done, the silence causes them to look at him curiously. He apparently is waiting for their attention.

He begins by addressing the congregation. "The words you just heard are not popular today. They call husband and wife to high standards of behavior. They present the clear demands of commitment. This passage lifts marriage from its romantic cultural setting and makes it a spiritual challenge. It refuses to accept the idea that the marriage relationship is a fair arrangement or some kind of a business agreement in which each party provides certain personal investments and gains certain benefits. As a covenant, marriage fits into a category of rare relationships. In fact, there's only one other relationship like it—and that's the relationship between Christ and His Bride, the Church."

Lowering his gaze slightly, the pastor now speaks directly to the couple. "As I have reminded you before, your marriage will not succeed if you think of it as a 50/50 equation in which each of you provides 50 percent in order to come up with a 100 percent marriage. What Paul is telling you in this passage is that marriage will require a 100 percent commitment from each of you."

He turns to the bride and says, "You as the wife get to submit to your husband." The audible intake of breath by the audience is frozen by his next words as he turns to the groom and says, "And you as the husband get to die for your wife."

Submission is a difficult concept to understand and accept in our culture today. The term has gotten a bad reputation and been confused with subservience. But if the word "submit" in

" The issues and challenges in marriage always get clearer (and harder) when we look at what Jesus did for the Church. "

Ephesians 5:22 has been misunderstood, the word "love" in verse 25 has been ignored and devalued. The truth is that if we allow the world to define either of these words, we will not be able to follow through with a Christian marriage.

We can start taking the Bible's teaching on marriage seriously only if we realize that the central idea behind the relationship between a husband and a wife has to do with the relationship between Christ and the Church. Christian marriages are designed to present a picture of Christ's love for the world. That's why Paul can write, "This mystery is profound, and I am saying that it refers to Christ and the church" (Eph. 5:32). The issues and challenges in marriage always get clearer (and harder) when we look at what Jesus did for the Church. This chapter begins with a command to imitate God and ends with the command to conduct our marriages as an imitation of Christ's relationship with His Bride, the Church.

Couples who fail to understand and agree to the biblical definitions of submission and love will encounter great difficulties in marriage. Their relationship will often be defined by a struggle of wills pitted against each other rather than a powerful combination of wills seeking to submit to God's will.

There's no shortage of twisted teachings on marriage, even among Christians. This passage is often handled haphazardly. Submission, however, does not mean accepting abuse, and leadership doesn't mean getting our own way all the time. Women who plead with men to lead in the family are frequently not asking their husbands to make all the decisions as much as they are asking their husbands to truly love them. When a woman knows that her husband loves her like Christ loved the Church, willing to die for her (and living that way), her resistance to submission melts away.

D. L. Moody used to say, "If I wanted to find out whether a man is a Christian, I wouldn't go to his minister. I'd go and ask his wife. If a man doesn't treat his wife right, I don't want to hear him talk about Christianity. What is the use of talking about salvation for the next life if he has no salvation for this? We want a Christianity that goes into our homes and into everyday lives."

D. L. Moody was echoing the Bible. Men who love are the key to a godly home. Fortunately, Jesus is just as willing to help us live out our marriages for Him as He is willing to help us imitate Him in other areas!

Express It

If you are in a marriage, think of ways you can set aside special time to pray for your mate and for your relationship. Invite Christ to become intertwined with both of you. Ask Him to help you understand your role and your mate's role. Commit to being the person He wants you to be in your marriage.

Consider It

As you read Ephesians 5:22–33, consider these questions:

1) In verse 22 Paul uses the word "submit"; in verse 33 he uses the word "respect." Both words describe the wife's role. How does "respect" help you understand "submit"?

_____

_____

_____

2) Define "submission" and "love" as Paul uses the words here.

_____

_____

_____

3) What in this passage keeps marriage from becoming a monarchy?

_____

_____

_____

4) How does this passage keep marriage from becoming a frustrating experiment in a democracy of two people?

_____

_____

_____

5) What part of this passage echoes the Great Commandment? (See Mark 12:29–31.)

_____

_____

_____

6) Compare verse 31 with Genesis 2:24 and Matthew 19:4–6. What conclusions do you draw from these passages?

_____

_____

_____

7) What challenge for marriage do you take personally from this passage?

_____

_____

_____

Honoring Christ

The testing and proving grounds of life skills usually involve home and work. If we learn to do well in those two environments, we can get along with almost anyone. We can function in almost any other situation. So, learning the lessons for home and work are crucial to "walking worthy of Christ."

Ephesians 6:1–9

Children and Parents

6 Children, obey your parents in the Lord, for this is right. ²"Honor your father and mother" (this is the first commandment with a promise), ³"that it may go well with you and that you may live long in the land." ⁴Fathers, do not provoke your children to anger, but bring them up in the discipline and instruction of the Lord.

Slaves and Masters

⁵Slaves, obey your earthly masters with fear and trembling, with a sincere heart, as you would Christ, ⁶not by the way of eye-service, as people-pleasers, but as servants of Christ, doing the will of God from the heart, ⁷rendering service with a good will as to the Lord and not to man, ⁸knowing that whatever good anyone does, this he will receive back from the Lord, whether he is a slave or free. ⁹Masters, do the same to them, and stop your threatening, knowing that he who is both their Master and yours is in heaven, and that there is no partiality with him.

> # Key Verse
>
> *Rendering service with a good will as to the Lord and not to man* (Eph. 6:7).

Go Deeper

A child's obeying a parent is part of God's plan and has always been a part of God's plan. Several passages in the Old Testament relate to children being obedient to their parents. (See Ex. 20:12, Deut. 5:16, Prov. 6:20 and 30:17.) In the New Testament, Colossians 3:20 as well as this Ephesians passage make the same point.

Ephesians 6:1–4 includes five reasons for child obedience. These are not human opinions but God's Word. The first reason why children should obey their parents is that doing so is a way to demonstrate obedience and gratitude to the Lord. He gave children their parents along with the command to honor them. The second reason children should obey their parents is that God says it is right (not necessarily convenient or fun).

A third reason children should obey their parents is that God requires such obedience in the Ten Commandments. Reason number four is found in Ephesians 6:3: "that it may go well with you." Children obey their parents because it brings good to them when they obey and not evil. And reason number five states that children who obey their parents are blessed with extended life—"that you may live long in the land."

When Paul wrote to the Ephesian church and the other churches around it, he wrote to the expected audience (leaders, husbands, wives and parents). But he also wrote to an unexpected audience (children and slaves). Paul knew that in those congregations there would be children and slaves who needed to hear his advice. So, Paul addressed them, and thus honored them, by expecting them, as he did the others, to act directly under God's instructions.

God uses our children to help us understand the difficulties that our parents experienced while raising us. Sometimes kids don't listen to us the way we want them to. Somebody has said that there are three ways to get things done: 1) You can do it yourself; 2) You can ask someone else to do it for you; or 3) You can ask your kids not to do it. In the heat of a contest of wills between parents and children, however, sometimes it's hard to see the humor.

A child's primary responsibility is to obey his or her parents. Paul immediately connects obedience with honor, using the language of the fifth commandment (Ex. 20:12, Deut. 5:16). The lesson here is not a demand for agreement but a command to respect and cooperate. This is easy when parents ask their children to do what children want to do. But it becomes a matter of trust and obedience to God when parents ask them to do what they don't want to do. Honor and respect don't ultimately depend on parents' *being* honorable but upon a child's acceptance of God's will.

The parents' responsibility is to make a community in their home that will enable children to respond in the way that they should. Ultimately, fathers bear the greater responsibility for the strength of the family. As part of a people being woven into a family, when our families are strong, we'll make strong churches. When we make strong churches, we'll make beautiful patterns that draw people to Christ.

God's directions for fathers include a negative command and two positive ones. Fathers are: 1) not to provoke their children to anger but are to 2) discipline them in the Lord and 3) instruct

> **"** *When our families are strong, we'll make strong churches. When we make strong churches, we'll make beautiful patterns that draw people to Christ.* **"**

them in the Lord (see Eph. 6:4). Children will get angry and need to learn how to deal with those emotions. But God's Word warns fathers about deliberately provoking kids to anger. On the other hand, children must remember who the adult is. Discipline has to do with correction and allowing children to discover the meaning of consequences. If they learn this lesson at home under our loving protection, they won't have to learn it in the harsh environment of the world.

Instruction has to do with teaching, talking and showing. It's true that in the home more is caught than taught, but both forms of learning need to be going on. Until we work on the "taught" part, we won't really know what's being "caught" by our children.

In Paul's day, the slave/master relationship was an extension of home life. When we talk about slavery in the context of American history, the term primarily means one race enslaving another race. But that's not the context of slavery in the Bible.

In the Old Testament, some of the slaves were Israelites— slaves to other Israelites. In the New Testament, a slave was anybody who got in the way of the Roman armies. A lot of the slaves were Jews. Many Christians were slaves. As the Roman armies moved across Europe, practically everyone who was in their path became a slave. The slaves Paul was addressing were people who had fallen victim to the might of another individual with little reference to race.

When Paul spoke to wives, he said, "Submit to your own husbands as to the Lord" (Eph. 5:22). When he spoke to husbands, he said, "Love your wives as Christ loved the Church" (Eph. 5:25). When he spoke to children, he said, "Obey your parents in the Lord." Now he speaks to servants and says, "Obey your earthly masters with . . . a sincere heart, as you would Christ."

Masters get the same basic instructions. We can't miss the pattern. When Paul is talking about the various members of the family of God, he is saying, "Whatever your station in life, you hold that station, but do it as unto the Lord." There is a deeper meaning to life than in just doing your job. There's a spiritual purpose in being a good child or a good employee.

The key verse for this lesson states a central rule for living as a follower of Jesus: We treat people who fill various roles in our lives as if Jesus were filling that role. As one person eloquently stated it, "When I can see Jesus standing right behind my parents, my children, my employees or my boss, I know I'm expected to treat each of them with the respect that Jesus perfectly deserves."

Express It

As you pray, spell out your gratitude to God for your parents and those who have served as masters in your life. Tell God what you think He has taught you through them. Ask Him for wisdom in carrying out your roles as parent and/or boss. Describe your understanding of your job description in relation to Him.

Consider It

As you read Ephesians 6:1–9, consider these questions:

1) What is it about a child's obedience to his or her parents that is "right"?

_____

_____

2) How do you understand the "honor" part of your relationship with your parents?

_____

_____

3) What promise did God connect with honor in the fifth commandment?

_____

_____

4) How important in the light of this passage is it for parents to carefully observe and take note of their children's individual personality, patterns and skills?

_____

_____

5) What words did Paul use to describe the expected attitude of a Christian slave toward his or her master? What do Paul's words mean for a work environment today?

_____

_____

6) In what ways were slaves serving the Lord while serving their masters?

_____

_____

7) What were the master's responsibilities if he or she was a believer?

_____

_____

8) How would Paul's instructions bring about good and cause serious damage to the institution of slavery?

_____

_____

Armed and Dangerous

If you are a believer in Jesus Christ, Satan considers you armed and dangerous. He will treat you as the enemy. And he won't fight fair. The devil is the ultimate terrorist. He will attack when you least expect it. Do you know how to use your spiritual equipment and weapons?

Ephesians 6:10–24

The Whole Armor of God

¹⁰Finally, be strong in the Lord and in the strength of his might. ¹¹Put on the whole armor of God, that you may be able to stand against the schemes of the devil. ¹²For we do not wrestle against flesh and blood, but against the rulers, against the authorities, against the cosmic powers over this present darkness, against the spiritual forces of evil in the heavenly places. ¹³Therefore take up the whole armor of God, that you may be able to withstand in the evil day, and having done all, to stand firm. ¹⁴Stand therefore, having fastened on the belt of truth, and having put on the breastplate of righteousness, ¹⁵and, as shoes for your feet, having put on the readiness given by the gospel of peace. ¹⁶In all circumstances take up the shield of faith, with which you can extinguish all the flaming darts of the evil one; ¹⁷and take the helmet of salvation, and the sword of the Spirit, which is the word of God, ¹⁸praying at all times in the Spirit, with all prayer and supplication. To that end keep alert with all perseverance, making supplication for all the saints, ¹⁹and also for me, that words may be given to me in opening my mouth boldly to proclaim the mystery of the gospel, ²⁰for which I am an ambassador in

chains, that I may declare it boldly, as I ought to speak.

Final Greetings

²¹So that you also may know how I am and what I am doing, Tychicus the beloved brother and faithful minister in the Lord will tell you everything. ²²I have sent him to you for this very purpose, that you may know how we are, and that he may encourage your hearts.

²³Peace be to the brothers, and love with faith, from God the Father and the Lord Jesus Christ. ²⁴Grace be with all who love our Lord Jesus Christ with love incorruptible.

> # Key Verse
>
> *Put on the whole armor of God, that you may be able to stand against the schemes of the devil* (Eph. 6:11).

Go Deeper

God's Word reveals to us certain patterns in Satan's tactics. He does not attack us when and where we are strong, but he waits for moments of weakness. When we stumble, he's right there. The acronym H.A.L.T. provides a warning to help us remember those times we can expect Satan to attack us. We need to exercise the most caution when we are Hungry, Angry, Lonely or Tired. That's when we need to halt and acknowledge God's presence. (See Ps. 46.)

When Jesus was *hungry,* Satan showed up to tempt Him (Matt. 4:1–11). Note what spiritual weapons Jesus used to repel Satan's

attack. Ephesians 4:27 warns us that *anger* gives an "opportunity to the devil." After forty days in the wilderness alone, we can expect that Jesus was experiencing *loneliness,* so Satan tempted Him thinking he could gain an advantage over Jesus. And Elijah was *tired* after a huge victory over 450 Baal priests and crumbled under the threat of one woman (1 Kings 18–19).

Whenever we find ourselves hungry, angry, lonely or tired, we need to halt and "be still and know that I am God" (Ps. 46:10). Our spiritual equipment won't help us if we don't learn to use it well.

We hear a great deal about spiritual warfare these days, but no one speaks to the subject with more authority than the apostle Paul. Throughout human history, warfare has been a prevalent reality, but the longest warfare of all has been the spiritual conflict between the forces of heaven and Satan's powers of hell. This is the ultimate battle—our ongoing conflict with Satan—a daily battle that we resume every morning and, hopefully, we put to rest every night. God's Word, however, tells us how to win these conflicts. We've been offered everything we need for victory.

When Paul talks about putting on the armor of God, he simply is describing a soldier of the Roman Empire. The apostle uses six metaphors derived directly from the armor that a Roman soldier wore in battle. The best way to understand how to make practical applications about these pieces of armor is to ask a series of questions:

Question 1: Are we genuinely sincere about fighting the devil? Ephesians 6:14 describes the girdle, or the heavy-duty belt, a soldier used. We don't wear this equipment unless we're going into battle. Paul relates this belt to fastening truth around our lives. Truthfulness is essential if we're going to fight the devil. A key word is *integrity*. If we're serious about fighting off the devil, then it's going to show up in our integrity.

Question 2: Are we really living the kind of life that enables us to engage in a conflict with Satan? Do we want to go to battle with Satan living the kind of life we lived yesterday? That's why Paul says that in addition to truth, we have to put on the breastplate of righteousness (6:14). The breastplate was that part of the armor that covered the front of the body from the neck down to the thighs. It was designed to protect a soldier's vital organs. Spiritually, the breastplate of righteousness is a devout and holy life marked by purity. Our spiritual vital organ—life itself—needs righteous protection.

❝Without the Word of God and your knowledge of it, you're not prepared to meet Satan today. And you won't be prepared to meet him tomorrow either.❞

Question 3: Are we prepared to fight? Do we have our feet shod with readiness that is derived from the gospel of peace (v. 15)? The Roman soldier used to wear sandals that had long, leather laces that would tie up around his ankle and calf. But more than that, these shoes were studded with sharp nails. One of the reasons why Julius Caesar was so successful as a general was the fact that his men wore military shoes that made it possible for them to cover long distances in short periods of time.

Just as their sandals gave Roman soldiers an advantage in battle, the gospel of peace gives Christians an advantage in our conflict with Satan. Believers can stand firm upon the truth that we have peace with God—a peace purchased through the death of His Son, Jesus.

Question 4: Are we able to defend ourselves against Satan's attacks? Part of our defense comes from the shield of faith (v. 16), by which we're able to quench all the fiery darts of the wicked one. Satan fires volleys of fiery lies, innuendoes, threats, and temptations at us that must be "extinguished" by faith, or our fighting days are over. Faith helps us ward off these deadly intruders.

Question 5: Is our head protected for a fight with Satan? Paul says in verse 17, "Take the helmet of salvation." That helmet was designed specifically to protect a soldier's head against lethal blows from his enemies. If we don't have God's salvation for our life, then Satan can attack our mind. Without a strong, renewed, Spirit-filled mind, we will be rendered useless as soldiers.

Question 6: Have we learned the art of offensive warfare? We can use the sword of God's Word to counterattack Satan (v. 17). Like learning to wield a steel sword, we all need to develop skill and understanding of the weapon God has issued to us, which will take time, practice, help and commitment.

That's our armor. Our armor is integrity, purity, peace, faith, salvation and the Word of God. When we are suited up with those pieces of armor, we have all that is necessary to win the battle against Satan. Verses 18–19 describe how we "march" through life—in constant communication with our captain, the Lord Jesus, in prayer.

Years ago, the Scottish pastor Thomas Guthrie said, "The Bible is an armory of heavenly weapons, a laboratory of infallible medicines, a mine of exhaustless wealth. It is a guidebook for every road, a chart for every sea, a medicine for every malady and a balm for every wound. Rob us of our Bible, and our sky has lost its sun." Without the Word of God and your knowledge of it, you're not prepared to meet Satan today. And you won't be prepared to meet him tomorrow either.

Express It

Paul begins this letter with prayer and closes it by asking his readers to pray. That was his pattern. His readers depended on him to give them sound teaching, and Paul evened the score by depending on them for prayer. Who prays for you regularly? For whom do you pray regularly? Have you agreed to be in a prayer partnership with anyone? As we endure spiritual warfare, we need to know others are supporting us in prayer, and we need to commit to supporting them also. Pray for some fellow Christian soldiers today.

Consider It

As you read Ephesians 6:10–24 , consider these questions:

1) What does it mean to "put on" God's armor?

_____

_____

_____

_____

2) Identify each of the pieces of armor, and describe how you've been trained to use it.

_____

_____

_____

_____

3) How does Paul describe the various aspects of our battle with Satan? What can we expect?

_____

_____

_____

_____

4) In what ways does a passage like this help you understand certain experiences in your life?

_____

_____

_____

_____

5) At what points in your life have you felt Satan's most severe attacks?

_____

_____

_____

_____

6) What new insight have you had about spiritual warfare in thinking about this passage?

_____

_____

_____

Lesson 13

A Living Tapestry

With the exception of the much longer letter to the Romans, Ephesians provides the most complete overview of God's plan for us in the New Testament. If we want to have a healthy view of the world around us and a triumphant experience in our Christian lives, we will have to live out the truth found in Ephesians. Are you ready?

Ephesians 4:1–6

Unity in the Body of Christ

4 I therefore, a prisoner for the Lord, urge you to walk in a manner worthy of the calling to which you have been called, ²with all humility and gentleness, with patience, bearing with one another in love, ³eager to maintain the unity of the Spirit in the bond of peace. ⁴There is one body and one Spirit—just as you were called to the one hope that belongs to your call— ⁵one Lord, one faith, one baptism, ⁶one God and Father of all, who is over all and through all and in all.

Key Verse

I therefore, a prisoner for the Lord, urge you to walk in a manner worthy of the calling to which you have been called (Eph. 4:1).

Go Deeper

The design of God's tapestry can be found in other places in His Word. Once we become aware of His plan, we see evidences of it everywhere! Notice the beautiful parallel between the outline of the Christian life in Ephesians and the themes introduced in the first psalm: "Blessed is the man who walks not in the counsel of the wicked, nor stands in the way of sinners, nor sits in the seat of scoffers; but his delight is in the law of the LORD, and on his law he meditates day and night" (Ps. 1:1–2).

The wise person doesn't walk in futility like the wicked but walks worthy of Christ's calling. He or she doesn't walk in darkness but walks as a child of light. He or she doesn't walk under the world's counsel but walks in love, as Christ walked.

The wise person doesn't take his stand with sinners but stands against the devil's schemes. He or she doesn't compromise with the world's values but deliberately puts on the whole armor of God because every part of that armor is essential in order to stand. He or she doesn't stand in the way of sinners lest they be confused and deceived but urges sinners to turn to Christ and walk in His love.

And the wise person doesn't sit with scoffers but sits with Christ in hope. Such people find their deepest delight in meditating on God's Word day and night, letting the truth fill them with wisdom. They live each day with profound gratitude that God has raised them with Christ and seated them with Him in the heavenly places in Christ Jesus.

Where you sit, walk and stand determine your spiritual health. When you sit, walk and stand with Christ, you are living as worthy strands in God's great tapestry.

One way to summarize this profound letter is to think about the seven great themes that are woven into the tapestry of Ephesians. Each builds upon the previous ones. But every theme can be seen in the final appearance of the whole. A tapestry can be examined for its individual colors and threads, but the full effect can't be felt until we step back and see the whole pattern. The themes of Ephesians give us the pattern of God's great plan, His great tapestry.

The first theme is the sovereign election by a loving, all-wise God (Eph. 1:3–23). Before time began, God made sure that nothing would inhibit our salvation. In His great sovereignty, He elected us to be holy saints. He gets the first and final word on the design and pattern of His tapestry.

The second theme tells why we need God's sovereign election (2:1–2). We are stillborn in sin; physically alive, to be sure, but born spiritually dead. We confirm we're sinners when we sin as soon as we get a chance! Until we acknowledge this, we can't rejoice in the wonder of God's election. Our souls must learn the truth of John Newton's words, "Amazing grace, how sweet the sound that saved a wretch like me. I once was lost but now am found; was blind but now I see." Alone we're just a lost strand of wool, but woven into God's tapestry we are made part of His grand design.

The third is our unity in Christ—a unity in His Church, the family of the graciously saved (2:4–3:21). Our unity in Christ is seen from God's perspective. If we look from the human side, we don't see a great deal of unity. But when we see God's side, God is blending us together in such a way that we are becoming a beautiful tapestry, rolled out across the ages.

The fourth theme is that we're to walk worthy of our calling (4:1–6). Once we have been placed into God's family, we're encouraged to act the part! We've chosen Ephesians 4:1 as the key verse for this summary lesson because it records the pivotal challenge of the letter. It demands our attention to all that God has already done for us and then makes us accountable to live up

"Someday we will stand in a place that allows us to see the breathtaking design from God's perspective. Then we will see what God has always seen."

to God's calling. God has created the tapestry and placed us in it. One of our regular self-examination questions ought to be, *Am I living worthy of all God has done for me?*

The fifth theme in this book is that unity does not destroy our diversity (4:7–16). We have various gifts and various offices in the Church, which prove that while we are different, we still maintain our diversity in the midst of this unity. The goal of creating unity while allowing diversity proves to be a far greater achievement than we could ever accomplish by our own efforts. Unless we are continuously humbling ourselves and submitting to Christ's lordship, we will not experience the unity and diversity He wants to create before the watching world.

The sixth theme tells us to live beyond the boundaries and the stereotypes of society because we are saved, set apart and one in Christ (5:21–6:9). We find our place in society, but we look well beyond the boundaries of society because we have a new life in Christ Jesus.

The final great theme in this book is that we must be properly suited up if we're going to do battle with Satan (6:10–20). Satan isn't going to allow God to weave this tapestry without a fight. But God has provided the members of His family with everything they need to defeat the devil in battle.

Perhaps being a part of God's tapestry puts us "too close to the forest to see the trees." But someday we will stand in a place that allows us to see the breathtaking design from God's perspective. Then we will see what God has always seen. We will understand what we couldn't understand among the fibers.

And we will be filled with inexhaustible reasons to say with Paul, "Blessed be the God and Father of our Lord Jesus Christ, who has blessed us in Christ with every spiritual blessing in the heavenly places" (Eph. 1:3). In heaven, God's tapestry will finally worship its Master with one voice.

As we conclude this survey of the letter to the Ephesians, we might want to remember this book as *The Walker's Guide to the Christian Adventure.* Ephesians also fits the title *A Photo Album of Life in the Family of God.* If you want to live a life worthy of Christ's invitation, you need to keep Ephesians close at hand.

Express It

As you pray, humbly consider the great mystery that you have been placed by Christ into God's family by faith. Tell God what you have learned in this study of Ephesians and describe how these lessons will affect the way you live. Pray for at least five other members of the family of God by name who are beyond your usual circle of concern.

Consider It

As you read Ephesians 4:1–6, consider these questions:

1) What three actions come to mind when you think about walking worthy of your calling in Christ?

_____

_____

_____

2) Why doesn't the Christian life get easier?

_____

_____

_____

3) What does "walking worthy" have to do with spiritual warfare?

_____

_____

_____

4) Since part of your walk will take you through battle zones, can you identify the equipment God has provided? (See Eph. 6:10–20.)

_____

_____

_____

5) How would you describe your present state of spiritual combat readiness?

_____

_____

_____

6) In what ways do the "ones" in 4:1–6 encourage you to walk boldly through life?

_____

_____

_____

7) How has this study of Ephesians most affected your spiritual outlook?

_____

_____

_____

Notes

Notes

Notes

Notes

Notes

Notes

Notes

Notes

Notes

Notes